Art Profiles
For Kids

MICHELANGELO

Mitchell Lane
PUBLISHERS

P.O. Box 196
Hockessin, Delaware 19707
Visit us on the web: www.mitchelllane.com
Comments? email us: mitchelllane@mitchelllane.com

ART PROFILES FOR KIDS

Titles in the Series

Antonio Canaletto

Claude Monet

Michelangelo

Paul Cézanne

Pierre-Auguste Renoir

Vincent van Gogh

Art Profiles
For Kids

MICHELANGELO

Jim Whiting

P.O. Box 196
Hockessin, Delaware 19707
Visit us on the web: www.mitchelllane.com
Comments? email us: mitchelllane@mitchelllane.com

Copyright © 2008 by Mitchell Lane Publishers. All rights reserved. No part of this book may be reproduced without written permission from the publisher. Printed and bound in the United States of America.

Printing   1   2   3   4   5   6   7   8   9

Library of Congress Cataloging-in-Publication Data
Whiting, Jim, 1943-
  Michelangelo / by Jim Whiting.
      p. cm.—(Art profiles for kids)
  Includes bibliographical references and index.
  ISBN 978-1-58415-562-1 (library bound)
  1. Michelangelo Buonarroti, 1475-1564—Juvenile literature. 2. Artists—Italy—Biography—Juvenile literature. I. Michelangelo Buonarroti, 1475–1564. II. Title.
  N6923.B9W52 2007
  709'.2—dc22
  [B]
                                                                2007000659

ABOUT THE AUTHOR: Jim Whiting has been a remarkably versatile and accomplished journalist, writer, editor, and photographer for more than 30 years. He has had the opportunity to see much of Michelangelo's work firsthand during the course of his travels and relishes the opportunity to convey the excitement and wonder that these works have generated in him. A voracious reader since early childhood, Mr. Whiting has written and edited over 200 nonfiction children's books. He lives in Washington State with his wife and two teenage sons.

ABOUT THE COVER: The images on the cover are paintings by the various artists in this series.

PHOTO CREDITS: pp. 3, 28—Super Stocks; all other images are the works of Michelangelo.

PUBLISHER'S NOTE: The facts on which this story is based have been thoroughly researched. Documentation of such research appears on page 46. While every possible effort has been made to ensure accuracy, the publisher will not assume liability for damages caused by inaccuracies in the data, and makes no warranty on the accuracy of the information contained herein.

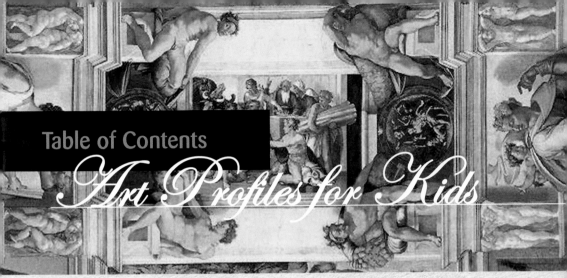

Table of Contents

Art Profiles for Kids

Chapter One
Discovering a Genius 7
For Your Information: The Medici 13

Chapter Two
Becoming Famous 15
For Your Information: Girolamo Savonarola 21

Chapter Three
The Sistine Chapel 23
For Your Information: Leonardo da Vinci 27

Chapter Four
Defending Florence 29
For Your Information: Resurrecting Rome 33

Chapter Five
Rome and St. Peter's 35
For Your Information: St. Peter's Basilica 41

Chronology 42
Timeline in History 43
Chapter Notes 44
Further Reading 45
    For Young Adults 45
    Works Consulted 45
    On the Internet 46
Glossary 47
Index 48

A Belgian merchant bought Michelangelo's *Madonna and Child* soon after its creation in 1504. He donated it to The Church of Our Lady in the city of Bruges, Belgium. It is the only statue of Michelangelo's to leave Italy while he was alive. Standing four feet high, the statue has had an adventurous history. Both Napoléon's and Hitler's soldiers "kidnapped" it. In both cases it was returned.

one

Discovering a Genius

Slowly the two horses picked their way along the rugged mountain road in north-central Italy. The route was winding and steep. The road wasn't in very good condition. Parts were muddy, some with large potholes. Rocks the size of fists—and even larger—were everywhere. The footing wasn't very secure.

Lodovico Buonarroti was riding one of the horses. Only about thirty years old at the time, he was a minor Italian nobleman who clung to a strong sense of family honor. The Buonarrotis had a long aristocratic heritage stretching back more than 250 years, but their fortunes had steadily shrunk. By now, Lodovico and his brother Francesco owned only a house in Florence and a small farm near the village of Settignano.

Lodovico considered working with his hands to be beneath his dignity. It had been a stroke of good fortune when he was appointed podestà (governor) of the small towns of Caprese and Chiusi, even though the appointment was for only six months.

Lodovico brought along his nineteen-year-old wife, Francesca, and their first child, Lionardo. Francesca was several months' pregnant with the couple's second child. She was already in frail health, so the journey was difficult for her.

Suddenly Francesca's horse stumbled over a rough place in the road. The abrupt movement caught her unaware and she fell off the horse.

Falling off a horse can lead to serious injury. Francesca was fortunate. Although she was shaken by the fall, her injuries were minor. The couple

Michelangelo's *David.* The artist wanted to emphasize David's bravery, so he depicted him at the moment he decided to fight the Philistine giant Goliath. The statue stands in the center of a large vaulted room in Florence's Galleria dell'Accademia, where tourists can walk completely around it and view it from any angle.

rested for a few days so that she could recover. Then they resumed the journey.

Several months later, Lodovico wrote, "Today this sixth of March [1475] . . . there was born to me a male child; I named him Michelangelo and he was born Monday morning before four or five o'clock and he was born when I was Podestà at Caprese . . . I had him baptized on the eighth of the same month in the Church of Santo Giovanni di Caprese."[1]

Lodovico had no idea that this was the first mention of a person who would become what many people consider the greatest artist of all time.

For some people, Francesca's survival and quick recovery—enabling her to give birth to Michelangelo—was a clear sign that God's hand had reached down to protect her. As Giorgio Vasari, one of Michelangelo's first biographers, wrote, "The benign ruler of heaven [God] graciously looked down on earth, saw the worthlessness of what was being done, the intense but utterly fruitless studies, and the presumption of men who were farther from true art than night is from day, and resolved to save us from our errors. So he decided to send into the world an artist who would be skilled in each and every craft, whose work alone would teach us how to attain perfection in design. . . . Moreover, he determined to give this artist the knowledge of true moral philosophy and the gift of poetic expression, so that everyone might admire and follow him as their perfect exemplar in life, work, and behavior and in every endeavor, and he would be acclaimed as divine."[2] Such a gifted person had to be protected while he was still inside his mother, waiting to be born.

Vasari wasn't alone in his admiration for Michelangelo. Nearly everyone who met him recognized his genius, which had begun to be apparent when he was still a teenager. When he died, he received the type of funeral customarily reserved for kings or popes of the Catholic Church.

Of course, Michelangelo's future fame and accomplishments were nowhere in evidence at his birth. In fact, Lodovico would have been shocked to know that his son would grow up to be an artist. Lodovico had little or no interest in art. He was a very practical man who looked down on artists. After all, they worked with their hands.

His lack of interest in the arts was somewhat unusual for his time, when Europe was going through the early stages of the Renaissance. The word *Renaissance* literally means "rebirth." It refers to the rebirth of classical ideals that reached back to the time of ancient Greece and Rome, many centuries earlier. These ideals were reflected in sculpture, painting, literature, architecture, and other forms of art. It was an exciting and stimulating time to be alive.

Nowhere was this more true than in Florence, one of the small city-states that dotted the Italian peninsula. These city-states competed fiercely with one another. With good reason, Florence was especially proud of its art. Many of the most famous Renaissance artists lived and worked in the city or the surrounding area.

These Florentine artists were supported by wealthy noblemen. Foremost was the powerful Medici (MEH-duh-chee) family. The Medici would play a key role in the development of Michelangelo's genius.

Michelangelo's birth came just before the end of Lodovico's term as podestà. It soon became apparent that Francesca couldn't nurse her new baby—it was too much of a strain on her health. Lodovico sent his new son to a nurse who lived near Settignano. Like most men in Settignano, the woman's husband worked in the stone quarries. Michelangelo later told Vasari, "Giorgio, if my brains are any good at all it's because I was born in the pure air of your Arezzo countryside, just as with my [nurse's] milk I sucked in the hammer and chisel I use for my statues."[3]

It's not clear how long Michelangelo lived with the stonecutter's family. His mother had three more sons—Buonarroto, Giovansimone, and Sigismondo—within the next six years. Each new child weakened her already delicate health. She died in 1481. Michelangelo spent considerable amounts of time in Settignano rather than with his widowed father in Florence. He gained experience using a hammer and chisel but did not yet attend school.

When Michelangelo was ten, Lodovico remarried and Michelangelo returned to Florence. His father wanted him to be educated, in preparation for a "respectable" career, such as a banker, merchant, or government

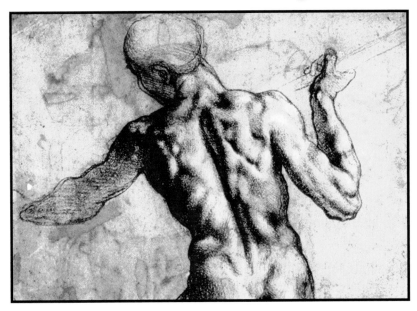

Michelangelo dissected corpses to learn how the human body was put together. He used this knowledge when he made sketches for his paintings. He used this sketch of a man to paint the female prophet, the Libyan Sibyl.

official. He hired a tutor for the boy. In three years, Michelangelo learned how to write and read but not much else.

Not much else, that is, except art. He often sneaked away from his lessons to draw what he saw around him. One of his close friends was Francesco Granacci. Francesco worked as an apprentice to a firm of family painters headed by Domenico Ghirlandaio, at the time the city's most popular and successful artist. He and his brothers made a good living by painting frescoes (FRES-kohz). Frescoes are a particular type of painting. First, the artist coats a surface with a thin layer of plaster, then quickly paints directly onto the wet plaster. The paint dries into the plaster. It is a delicate, painstaking process.

Francesco urged Michelangelo to join him. Michelangelo was only too eager to drop out of school and become an apprentice. His father didn't

approve. There were furious arguments, and sometimes Michelangelo was even beaten.

Michelangelo's intense desire to join Ghirlandaio was among the first demonstrations of one of his most characteristic qualities. He was very stubborn. Once he had made up his mind about something, it was often impossible to get him to change it.

Michelangelo finally wore down his father's resistance. In April 1488, Lodovico signed a three-year apprenticeship agreement with Ghirlandaio.

According to art historian Bernard Berenson, Michelangelo made the right choice. "The penwork in these early drawings, and indeed more than one trick of shorthand of later date, tell truthfully that Ghirlandaio was the man who first put a pen into Michelangelo's hand and taught him how to use it,"[4] he wrote.

Michelangelo proved to be a very quick study. According to Vasari, "The way Michelangelo's talents and character developed astonished Domenico, who saw him doing things quite out of the ordinary for boys of his age and not only surpassing his many other pupils but also very often rivaling the achievements of the master himself. On one occasion it happened that one of the young men studying with Domenico copied in ink some draped figures of women from Domenico's own work. Michelangelo took what he had drawn and, using a thicker pen, he went over the contours of one of the figures and brought it to perfection; and it is marvelous to see the difference between the two styles and the superior skill and judgment of a young man so spirited and confident that he had the courage to correct what his teacher had done."[5]

Incidents such as these may have made Ghirlandaio realize that he didn't have much to teach his headstrong young pupil. Yet he needed to find something for him to do for the next three years.

Not far away, Lorenzo de' Medici was about to make a decision that would solve Ghirlandaio's problem.

The Medici

The powerful Medici family traces its ancestry back to the thirteenth century. Scholars guess that the name comes from *medico*, which could suggest the earliest members were physicians.

Giovanni di Bicci de' Medici entered the banking industry around the early 1400s. Before the family's rise to power, only wealthy landowners had any political power. Now it became possible to rise in importance by doing well in business.

Under Cosimo the Elder (1389–1464), the Medici became the dominant family in Florence. While Cosimo didn't hold any official position, he was the city's leading citizen. He had great wealth and the respect of his fellow citizens. Lorenzo the Magnificent, Cosimo's grandson, became the most famous of the Medici rulers. He was especially associated with the flowering of the arts that made Florence the center of the Renaissance. Lorenzo's successors were not as gifted as he was. Cosimo's direct line ended with the assassination of the very unpopular Alessandro de' Medici in 1537.

The "junior" branch—which was descended from Cosimo the Elder's younger brother Lorenzo—then took over the family fortunes. Duke Cosimo I (1519–1574) restored the family's reputation and power. But the Medici began a steady decline after his death, though Cosimo's grandson Cosimo II was an early supporter of the famous scientist Galileo Galilei. Gian-Gastone de' Medici (1671–1737) left no male heirs. He was the last of the line.

Statue of Giuliano de' Medici
c. 1526–1534

The family's most enduring legacy is in art and architecture. In addition to Michelangelo, they also supported many other notable craftsmen. Their art collection became the basis for the Uffizi in Florence, one of the world's foremost art museums. The Medici also contributed three Popes: Leo X, Clement VII, and Leo XI.

Men weren't the only important Medici. When Catherine de Medici (1519–1589) married the future French king Henry II in 1533, she brought the ideals of the Renaissance to France with her. She is also credited with introducing high heels. She was a short woman who wanted to appear taller.

Michelangelo's *Pietà* was his first major sculpture. It is about six feet wide at the base and more than five feet high. Mary actually appears to be younger than her son. Some scholars believe that Michelangelo intended this youthful appearance to reflect her virginity and purity.

two

Becoming Famous

In the 1480s, Lorenzo was the leader of the Medici. Probably the greatest member of this wealthy and powerful family, he was also known as Lorenzo the Magnificent.

For decades, the Medici had been collecting classical art, especially Greek and Roman statues. They displayed the statues in an outdoor garden called San Marco. As the collection grew, Lorenzo thought it was too bad that no one in Florence was producing sculpture of that quality. The last great Florentine sculptor was Donatello, and he had been dead for more than two decades.

One reason may simply have been how hard and messy it is to sculpt. As Leonardo da Vinci described the process, "The sculptor in creating his work does so by the strength of his arm by which he consumes the marble, or other obdurate [hard] material in which his subject is enclosed: and this is done by most mechanical exercise, often accompanied by great sweat which mixes with the marble dust and forms a kind of mud daubed all over his face. The marble dust flours him all over so that he looks like a baker; his back is covered with a snowstorm of chips, and his house is made filthy by the flakes and dust of stone."[1] The craft also demanded almost absolute perfection. If a sculptor made a mistake by chipping away too much material, there was no way of putting it back.

In 1489, Lorenzo decided to do something to give sculpting in Florence a boost. He established a new school of sculpture. The head was Bertoldo di Giovanni, a pupil of the great Donatello.

Lorenzo asked some of the city's leading artists to recommend promising young men to enter the school. For Ghirlandaio, this invitation offered an ideal opportunity to let Michelangelo move on. For Michelangelo, it was the chance of a lifetime. He quickly came to the attention of Lorenzo himself. The great man treated Michelangelo almost as a member of his extended family. He gave him a room in the Medici palace, took care of all his meals, and paid him a monthly salary.

Perhaps just as important, Michelangelo was allowed to join the stimulating discussions that took place in the Medici household. He was exposed to Greek and Roman literary classics. He even learned how to write sonnets, a particular type of poem. He would express many of the important events of his life in sonnet form. Scholars believe that he achieved the same level of distinction in his poetry as he did in the other art forms that he employed.

In short, Michelangelo was getting the full education he hadn't received as a boy. He would later regard the time he spent in the Medici household as the happiest period of his life.

The students didn't spend all their time sculpting. They also studied the works of the great Italian painters such as Giotto and Masaccio, observing them and then copying what they saw. Once, when competition among students became particularly intense, Michelangelo and Pietro Torrigiano resorted to fistfighting.

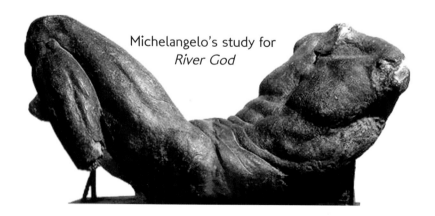

Michelangelo's study for
River God

"When we were boys," Torrigiano said years later, he and Michelangelo would "go into the Church of the Carmine to learn drawing from the chapel of Masaccio. It was [Michelangelo's] habit to banter [tease] all who were drawing there; and one day, when he was annoying me, I got more angry than usual, and, clenching my fist, I gave him such a blow on the nose that I felt bone and cartilage go down like biscuit beneath my knuckles; and this mark of mine he will carry with him to the grave."[2]

Vasari tells a very different version of the incident. "It is said that Torrigiano, who had struck up a friendship with Michelangelo, then became jealous on seeing him more honored than himself and more able in his work. At length Torrigiano started to mock him, and then he hit him on the nose so hard that he broke and crushed it and marked Michelangelo for life."[3]

Whichever story is closer to the truth, one thing is certain. It was a very harsh blow. "Michelangelo was carried home as a dead man,"[4] notes art historian Rona Goffen. This obvious distortion of his facial features would haunt him for the rest of his life. He was always conscious of how his smashed nose disfigured his face. He was often depressed about his appearance.

Within three years of entering the school, Michelangelo had produced his first sculpture, *Madonna of the Stairs*. It depicts an especially warm relationship between the biblical mother Mary and the baby Jesus. Michelangelo would often return to this theme. Some scholars believe that it represented the mother's love he never enjoyed as a little boy. *The Battle of the Centaurs* followed the next year. Both works were highly regarded by his contemporaries.

This promising start hit a roadblock in 1492 when Lorenzo died and his oldest son, Piero, succeeded him as head of the Medici family. Piero was an arrogant young man who despised Michelangelo. The artist realized he was no longer welcome at the Medici home and returned to his father's house. Soon he met the prior of the Santo Spirito church in Florence. At the time, dissection of the human body was illegal and even punishable by death. Even so, Michelangelo persuaded the prior to allow him to study

Bacchus was the Roman god of wine. Michelangelo carved him to appear as if he has had a bit much to drink. Behind Bacchus is a faun that is sneaking grapes.

the corpses of people awaiting burial. He would sneak into the church at night, light a candle so that he could see what he was doing, cut into the cadavers using kitchen knives he had smuggled from home, and leave well before dawn. As a result of these nighttime studies, he learned how muscles produce movement.

With his new knowledge, he became the foremost artist in terms of depicting the human body, which represented perfection to him. He created many statues and paintings in which the subjects are nude.

Two years after Lorenzo died, Piero had alienated the people of Florence so much that he was driven from the city. Mobs looted the Medici palace. Michelangelo feared that the anti-Medici feelings could be dangerous for anyone connected with the family—which he definitely was. He fled to the city of Bologna and stayed there for a year.

When he returned to Florence in 1495, a monk named Girolamo Savonarola had become dominant in the city. People lived in fear of him. He opposed any form of art that didn't promote Catholic beliefs. Michelangelo couldn't stand this attitude. To him, he said, this kind of art was appropriate only "for women, especially old or very young women, as well as for monks, nuns, and certain aristocrats, who are insensible to true harmony."[5]

Nonetheless, Michelangelo was able to get a few commissions. One would change his life. His patron, Lorenzo di Pierfrancesco de' Medici (a distant cousin of Lorenzo the Magnificent's), suggested that he create a statue of Cupid in the ancient Roman style. He could pass it off as an

antique and make some good money. The plot backfired. The purchaser, Cardinal Raffaele Riario, realized it was a fraud. But the quality of the workmanship impressed him. He wrote to Michelangelo and invited him to come to Rome, assuring him that he would be able to find work there as a sculptor. Michelangelo accepted the invitation and arrived in Rome in the early summer of 1496.

He soon made his mark. His first work was a statue of Bacchus, the Roman god of wine. It shows classical influences, yet it also shows human emotion, which few sculptors had managed to portray well.

Something far greater was just around the corner. In 1498, Michelangelo received a commission to create a Pietà (pee-ay-TAH). Coming from a word that means "pity," it was any piece of art that depicted the Virgin Mary holding the dead body of her son, Jesus.

It took him about a year to complete the statue. Michelangelo drew on his knowledge of anatomy to create a vivid, realistic Jesus. Mary gazes down on his body. Rather than sadness, her face seems to show an acceptance of things as they are. It is the most finished sculpture he ever created. Every detail is perfectly realized. He even made some of the clothing so thin that the marble is almost transparent.

The work created a sensation. It revealed that at the relatively young age of twenty-four, he was one of the most important artists of his era.

It also showed how strong an ego that Michelangelo had. One day as he stood near the statue, he heard some onlookers wonder who had carved it. That night he returned with a lantern, hammer, and chisel and carved his name onto a thin belt that crossed Mary's chest. It was the only work he ever signed. Soon he would become so well known that no one would ever again stand in front of one of his statues and wonder who had carved it.

In 1501 he returned to Florence. He missed his family. And there was another compelling reason. Several decades earlier, a sculptor named Agostino di Duccio had received a commission to make a statue from a giant block of marble. His work was a disaster. Most people considered that he had ruined the block. Called *The Giant*, it lay idle for years. Now

the church wanted someone else to try to produce something from it. Michelangelo was selected. He decided to carve David, the victor in the biblical battle of David and the giant Goliath. David slays the giant using his slingshot and a single stone. He then uses Goliath's sword to cut off his enemy's head.

The conflict was a common theme in art and sculpture. Nearly everyone portrayed the outcome of the battle with David standing in triumph, one foot on the severed head of Goliath. Michelangelo put his own spin on the theme by portraying David just before the fatal shot. David holds the sling almost casually over his left shoulder, while his right hand cups the stone. It shows him as being wary yet confident. It was an appropriate symbol for the city of Florence, and when Michelangelo completed it in 1504, nearly all the citizens were pleased. The *David* was immediately considered a treasure of Florence and stamped Michelangelo as the greatest sculptor in Italy.

There was at least one critic of the piece. A civic official told Michelangelo that David's nose was too big. Michelangelo used the statue's fourteen-foot height to trick the official. He stood on a platform at the level of the nose and chipped away a few bits of marble. The bits came from an area next to the nose that could have used a little bit of smoothing anyway. The official was so far below that he couldn't tell the difference, but he still congratulated Michelangelo for his "improvement."

For the rest of his life, Michelangelo would never have any problems finding work. That was good news for his family. None of them had done very well in life. They were constantly asking Michelangelo for money. He hardly ever turned them down, although he often complained.

He also began buying pieces of property in and near Florence. Even though he had defied his father by working with his hands, he had inherited his father's desire to be thought of as an important person. These purchases helped him achieve that social status.

Girolamo Savonarola

Girolamo Savonarola was born to a family of aristocrats in 1452. He was very bright and began studying philosophy and medicine. In 1474 he heard a sermon that changed his life. The sermon emphasized the wickedness of the world. Savonarola came to believe that to get to heaven, people not only had to renounce their sins, but also renounce the things of this world and lead a pure, simple life.

Savonarola became a monk and began preaching. When he stopped in Florence in 1482, he didn't make much of an impression. However, he returned in 1489, and this time had a much stronger influence. His sermons against the sinfulness of Florence attracted a great following. Many people regarded him as an inspired prophet. Even though his emphasis on religion was in direct opposition to the humanism of the Medici, the two sides managed to get along.

When Lorenzo de' Medici died in 1492, Savonarola urged the people to rise up against Piero de' Medici, who proved to be a poor successor to Lorenzo. In 1494, Piero was driven from the city. Savonarola proclaimed the city to be a republic ruled by Jesus Christ, and he urged the people to give up their excesses. They flocked to the center of the city, throwing things like poetry books and expensive clothing into massive bonfires.

Pope Alexander VI became alarmed at Savonarola's growing influence. He summoned him to Rome in 1495, but Savonarola refused to make the trip. He was convinced that the Pope would imprison him. Though the Pope ordered him to stop preaching, Savonarola ignored the command.

Two years later, the Pope excommunicated Savonarola—meaning he threw him out of the Catholic Church. By this time, many Florentines were becoming dissatisfied with Savonarola's strict rule.

The following year, he was taken prisoner, tortured, and placed on trial. He and two other monks were hanged on May 23, 1498, "on account of the enormous crimes of which they had been convicted."[6] The bodies were burned. A plaque in Florence's central city square marks the exact spot.

Girolamo Savonarola, painted by Fra Bartolomeo in 1498

An overall view of the Sistine Chapel shows how difficult Michelangelo's task was. He painted the entire ceiling and the semicircular designs that surround the windows on the top levels of the walls. The project took more than four years to complete.

three

The Sistine Chapel

The year that *David* was completed, Florence's city council decided to commission two huge murals to show heroic battle scenes that demonstrated the city's glory. They asked another famous artist, Leonardo da Vinci, to do one. Six months later, with the *David* triumphantly done, they asked Michelangelo to do the other.

It would have been a classic competition: two of the greatest artists of the Renaissance producing paintings facing each other. The project was never completed. Leonardo became frustrated with his technique, which involved a kind of varnish that caused the paint to drip off. He quit.

Michelangelo created a sketch, or initial drawing, but he didn't even have time to start to paint. In 1505, the new Pope Julius II summoned him to Rome. The Pope, who had a high opinion of himself, wanted Michelangelo to create a mammoth tomb in which he could be buried. He wanted it to be similar to the ones used by ancient Roman emperors. This commission would dog Michelangelo for the next four decades.

Michelangelo spent several months designing the tomb. It was huge: 24 feet wide, 36 feet deep, and nearly three stories high. The first level would depict bound prisoners, representing the Pope's conquests. The second level would have four huge statues, including Moses and St. Paul, two of the Church's most important figures. The other two would illustrate two aspects of Julius's personality. One would represent his quiet, thoughtful life, while the other would be lively, demonstrating the active side of the Pope's character. Smaller statues would adorn the tomb as

The scenes on the Sistine Chapel ceiling depict stories from the Bible. In the *Creation of Adam*, God is reaching out to give the spark of life to Adam.

well. A marble casket that would contain the Pope's remains would sit at the very top of the monument.

The only suitable place for his tomb, the Pope felt, was St. Peter's Basilica in Rome. Even so, he thought the church wasn't grand enough. He commissioned Donato Bramante to design a much larger version.

According to many historians, hiring Bramante created another problem. Bramante didn't like Michelangelo. He wanted to replace him as uppermost in the Pope's mind. He convinced Julius that it was bad luck to build a tomb while he was still alive.

It soon became difficult for Michelangelo to see the Pope. The last straw came one day in 1506 when a servant turned him away from the Pope's residence. Michelangelo replied, "You may tell the Pope that from now on, if he wants me, he can look for me elsewhere."[1]

"Elsewhere" proved to be Florence. Angrily, Julius ordered Michelangelo to return. He even threatened to invade Florence if Michelangelo didn't obey his orders. It was not an idle threat. The ambassador from Venice wrote of Julius, "It is virtually impossible to describe how strong and violent and difficult to manage he is. In body and

soul he has the nature of a giant. Everything about him is on a magnified scale, both his undertakings and passions."[2] A Spanish ambassador was even more blunt. "In the hospital in Valencia [a city in Spain] there are a hundred people chained up who are less mad than [Pope Julius]."[3]

Finally, Michelangelo went to Bologna, Italy, late in 1506 and apologized to the Pope. The Pope asked the sculptor to create a ten-foot-high bronze statue of him for that city. Michelangelo spent the next year working on the statue, and it was erected early in 1508.

Michelangelo returned to Rome to find that the Pope had a new assignment for him. Julius wanted him to paint the ceiling of the Sistine Chapel, which was situated near St. Peter's Basilica. The chapel had been built by Julius's uncle, Pope Sixtus IV. The side walls contained frescoes by some of the most famous artists of the time, but the ceiling had only stars. Julius wanted something more impressive.

"Painting is not my trade,"[4] Michelangelo protested. He was also suspicious of Bramante, who knew that Michelangelo had almost no experience with fresco painting. Michelangelo thought that Bramante wanted him to fail so that the commission would go to a rising young painter named Raphael, a friend of Bramante's. Even worse, Michelangelo was afraid that he would seem like a fool to the Pope. He might even lose some of his sculpting commissions.

The Pope overruled Michelangelo's objections. He did, however, promise that Michelangelo could return to his beloved sculpture when the project was completed. The artist got in one final jibe. He signed the contract to paint the ceiling as "I, Michelangelo, sculptor."[5]

Julius's original plan was relatively simple. He envisioned twelve figures, representing the twelve apostles. Michelangelo went far beyond this concept. Art historian Robin Richmond explains: "[Michelangelo] decided that Julius's plan was too banal and simple. The formality of the design would not use his talent for depicting the unclothed human form at all and his powers as an artist would be severely restricted."[6]

Michelangelo decided to have nine central panels, each depicting a scene from the biblical book of Genesis. These panels would be

surrounded by prophets, sibyls (legendary women prophets), and further scenes from the Old Testament. It was far grander than Julius had intended. The man who had originally balked at creating 12 figures was now committed to producing more than 300.

He built a scaffold and set to work. At first progress was slow. The ceiling was damp, so the paint wouldn't dry properly. It was very hard work. He had to grind and mix his own paint. Then he would stand for hours on end, leaning back and holding his brush overhead. Sometimes paint would drip into his face. He was also bitter because the painting consumed all his time and energy. There was no opportunity to work on his beloved sculptures. The Pope was constantly under his feet. Sometimes he inspected the work on a daily basis. He kept urging Michelangelo to work faster.

Once Michelangelo wanted to take some time off to visit Florence for an important feast day. According to Vasari, the Pope said, "'Well, what about this chapel? When will it be finished?'

" 'When I can, Holy Father,' said Michelangelo.

"Then the Pope struck Michelangelo with a staff he was holding and repeated: 'When I can! When I can! What do you mean? I will soon make you finish it.' "[7]

Finally Michelangelo was done. It was a staggering achievement. Everyone realized that the ceiling was a masterpiece when the chapel opened on November 1, 1512. It had a great deal of influence on the way that other people would paint.

The Pope died four months later. Michelangelo met with Julius's family, the della Roveres. Now that Julius was dead, the family was insistent that Michelangelo complete the tomb project. He concentrated on the project for more than three years, and during this time completed the statue of Moses. It is considered one of his most impressive achievements.

But once again the Medici family was about to exert a major influence on Michelangelo's life.

Leonardo da Vinci

The famous artist and inventor Leonardo was born in 1452 in a farmhouse in the village of Anchiano, about two miles from the town of Vinci. When he was fourteen, he went to Florence, where he became an apprentice for an artist named Andrea del Verrocchio. Verrocchio taught young Leonardo a great deal about different art forms.

His apprenticeship ended in 1472. His first known independent work, a drawing depicting the Arno River valley, dates from the following year. He continued to live and work in Florence for the next decade. In 1482, he moved to Milan. Shortly before leaving Milan in 1499, he completed *The Last Supper*, one of his most famous paintings.

He traveled extensively through Italy for the next seventeen years, rarely spending more than a few years in any one location. It was during this period (1503–1506) that he created the *Mona Lisa*, one of the most famous portraits ever painted.

King Francis I of France invited Leonardo to move to the town of Amboise, France, in 1516. He died there three years later.

Leonardo was more than a painter. He was also a notable sculptor. He was very interested in science and mathematics as well. His drawing *Vitruvian Man*, a classic illustration of the proportions of a human body, reveals his knowledge of anatomy. He was a military architect and engineer. He was a prolific inventor, drawing plans for many modern inventions such as parachutes, helicopters, machine guns, and calculators. The technology of his time simply wasn't advanced enough to allow his ideas to actually be built.

Leonardo recorded many of his observations in notebooks. These notebooks have become especially prized by collectors. Microsoft cofounder Bill Gates paid $30 million for one of them.

Today, Leonardo's reputation is as high as Vasari described it more than 400 years ago: "Marvelously endowed by heaven with beauty, grace, and talent in such abundance that he leaves other men far behind."[8]

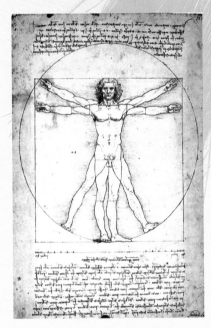

Vitruvian Man

In his later life, Michelangelo painted a few self-portraits. By then he had become successful and famous. Yet these portraits showed him in melancholy moods, which reflected his doubts about his spiritual well-being.

four

Defending Florence

Julius's replacement as Pope was Leo X, who had been born Giovanni di Lorenzo de' Medici, the second son of Lorenzo the Magnificent. Leo had known Michelangelo when he'd lived with the Medici, though they hadn't been particularly close.

Leo was upset that Michelangelo was working on something to glorify an important rival family. He wanted Michelangelo to spend his time honoring the Medici family. He asked him to design the facade of the Church of San Lorenzo in Florence, the home church of the Medici. For Michelangelo, who had no experience as an architect, it would be a new venture.

Starting in 1517, he threw himself into the project with his usual energy. His goal was to create the most magnificent building in Florence—and beyond. "With God's help, I will create the finest work in all Italy,"[1] he said.

Once again, Michelangelo had to halt work on the Julius tomb. With Leo's aid, he signed a new contract with the della Roveres. It called for a smaller, less ambitious tomb.

Michelangelo ran into problems with his new project. The Pope insisted that the marble come from a distant quarry. Just to get the marble to Florence, a long road would have to be built across the mountains in central Italy. When the road was finished, much of the marble that arrived was damaged. In 1520, the Pope canceled the contract. While

Michelangelo might have felt he had just wasted three years, the time and effort he put in helped to develop his architectural style.

Leo didn't give up on Michelangelo. The Pope's younger brother Guiliano had died in 1516. Three years later, his nephew Lorenzo also died. He asked Michelangelo to design tombs for the young men and a chapel that would contain the tombs.

Before Michelangelo got very far on these projects, Leo died. The new pope, Adrian VI, came from The Netherlands. He was allied with the della Roveres. He also disapproved of "pagan" statues, statues that—like Michelangelo's—reflected the style of ancient classical works.

Fortunately for Michelangelo, Adrian served for only twenty months before he died. The new pope was Giulio de' Medici, who became Pope Clement VII. He and Michelangelo had been good friends. He was much more sensitive to the artist's moods. He not only ordered Michelangelo to resume working on the chapel but added yet more work: the Laurentian Library, next to the Church of San Lorenzo. The library would house all the works of the Medici family.

In the meantime, Michelangelo was being sued by the della Roveres because he still hadn't finished the tomb for Julius. With the new pope's assistance, the family agreed to have Michelangelo build an even smaller tomb. When Michelangelo submitted the drawings, they were rejected. The lawsuit dragged on. "I desire to free myself from this obligation more than to live . . . I am completely out of my mind,"[2] Michelangelo wrote.

In spite of this distraction, he worked hard and diligently on the Medici projects. Then events outside his control intervened.

For years, northern Italy had been a battleground between the forces of King Francis I of France and Charles V, the Holy Roman Emperor. In 1527, Charles seemed to be on the verge of victory. The Pope was afraid that if that happened, Charles would try to conquer all of Italy—including Rome. He made a secret deal with Francis, but Charles found out and attacked Rome. Pope Clement had to flee. Charles's troops went on a rampage when they captured the city. They destroyed many priceless monuments and even turned their animals loose in the Sistine Chapel.

The Last Judgment, a fresco on one wall of the Sistine Chapel. Michelangelo depicted St. Bartholomew, one of Jesus' twelve disciples, who was skinned alive. He showed the saint holding his flayed skin, though Michelangelo included his own face instead of Bartholomew's.

Fortunately, the frescoes on the walls and Michelangelo's ceiling remained undamaged.

After the fighting in Rome, the Medici fled Florence, and the citizens there proclaimed a republic. They put pressure on Charles, who agreed to peace with Clement in 1529. As a Medici, Clement wanted his family restored to power. Charles even offered him some soldiers to help out.

Michelangelo was caught in the middle. He felt loyalty to the Medici family and to the city. He chose the city, volunteering to help improve the city's defenses. The fortifications he designed were too strong to be

overcome by direct attack. Clement decided to starve the city into submission. The siege lasted ten months, and even then it surrendered only after it was betrayed by one of the city's leading citizens. The furious Clement immediately executed many of the city's leaders. Fearing for his life, Michelangelo went into hiding.

He was fortunate. As the contemporary biographer Condivi describes the situation, "When Clement's fury abated, he wrote to Florence ordering that a search should be made for Michelangelo, and adding that when he was found, if he agreed to go on working at the Medicean monuments, he should be left at liberty and treated with due courtesy. On hearing news of this, Michelangelo came forth from his hiding place, and resumed the statues in the sacristy of San Lorenzo, moved thereto more by fear of the Pope than by love of the Medici."[3]

He was overworked, and his friends feared for his life. The Pope himself stepped in. He threatened to excommunicate Michelangelo unless he abandoned all but the most necessary work. Clement also helped in the ongoing della Rovere lawsuit. In 1532, Michelangelo negotiated still another version of the Julius tomb.

Although a little relieved, he wasn't happy. His favorite brother Buonarroto died in 1527. His father followed four years later. Michelangelo was now in his fifties, which by the standards of the times was fairly old. He was also haunted by all the work he had left uncompleted—in particular, the Julius tomb.

He had another, potentially more dangerous problem. Alessandro de' Medici had become the head of the family in Florence. For some reason, Alessandro hated Michelangelo. Many scholars believe that the only reason Michelangelo remained alive was because the Pope, as Alessandro's relative, had some influence on him. Clement became seriously ill in the spring of 1534. Michelangelo fled to Rome soon afterward, fearing that with Clement's death, his protection from Alessandro would disappear. He arrived in Rome on September 23. Clement died two days later. Michelangelo would never return to Florence.

Resurrecting Rome

At the height of the Roman Empire, it was almost literally true that "All roads lead to Rome." It was the most important city in the Western world. Roman emperors controlled much of Europe and even part of North Africa. The city was packed with impressive public buildings and works of art. It was also packed with people. Estimates of its population run as high as 1.5 million people. It would be nearly two thousand years before cities would again have as many people.

Over the centuries, Rome's political power and influence declined. While it always retained some of its earlier importance because it was the center of the Catholic Church, fewer and fewer people actually lived there. Scholars estimate that the population of Rome was only about 40,000 when Julius II became pope in 1503. The area in which they lived was less than one fourth its original size. Nearly all of the ancient structures lay in ruins. Cows and sheep grazed where famous people such as Julius Caesar had once walked. Sanitary facilities were very primitive. The city stank.

A servant to a pope, Poggius, witnessed Rome in its fallen state. In 1430, he noted: "This spectacle of the world, how is it fallen! how changed! how defaced! The path of victory is obliterated by vines, and the benches of the senators are concealed by a dunghill. . . . Seek among the shapeless and enormous fragments the marble theatre, the obelisks, the colossal statues, the porticos of Nero's palace: survey the other hills of the city, the vacant space is interrupted only by ruins and gardens. . . . The public and private edifices, that were founded for eternity, lie prostrate, naked, and broken, like the limbs of a mighty giant."[4]

Julius II wanted to make the Church much more influential in European affairs, so that once again, all roads would lead to Rome. The city would have to be rebuilt. He hired Bramante, Michelangelo, and other talented artisans to begin the process. While he didn't live long enough to see the results, Rome today is once again one of the world's most important cities.

Portrait of Julius II by Raphael

33

Standing nearly eight feet high, Michelangelo's statue of Moses was intended to become part of the tomb for Pope Julius II. Moses clutches the Ten Commandments in his right arm. The horns on his head represent a mistranslation of the Bible. The Hebrew term means "rays of light."

five

Rome and St. Peter's

Michelangelo's situation improved once he moved to Rome. He resumed his close friendship with a young nobleman named Tommaso de Cavalieri, and he met Vittoria Colonna. Now that he was older, he was more concerned about the salvation of his soul. According to his religious beliefs, he would not go to heaven unless his soul was "saved." Part of seeking salvation was asking forgiveness for one's sins. Vittoria helped him in that regard. She was a woman of strong and deeply held religious convictions. Scholars believe that she was the only woman who had a significant influence on Michelangelo.

He also hoped that he could finally finish the tomb of Julius, now that he was free of the Medici influence. The new pope, Paul III, a member of the Farnese family, had other ideas. Soon after his accession, Paul summoned Michelangelo. As Vasari explains, "After paying him compliments and making him various offers [the Pope] tried to persuade him to enter his service and remain near him. Michelangelo refused, saying that he was bound under contract to the duke of Urbino until the tomb of Julius was finished. Then the Pope grew angry and said: 'I have nursed this ambition for thirty years, and now that I'm Pope am I not to have it satisfied? I shall tear the contract up. I'm determined to have you in my service, no matter what.'"[1]

Despite the Pope's insistence, the contract remained in force. But the artist couldn't ignore Paul's wishes. Once again Michelangelo had to paint for a pope.

Paul wanted Michelangelo to do two more frescoes in the Sistine Chapel. One, *The Last Judgment*, would be done on the wall behind the altar. The other, *Fall of the Rebel Angels*, would be applied to the entrance wall. For some reason, Michelangelo never painted the latter.

Because Clement had considered commissioning *The Last Judgment*, Michelangelo had made a number of preliminary sketches. Now, in 1535, he began in earnest. The fresco depicted a dramatic change for Michelangelo. The old Renaissance faith in the power and wisdom of human nature, so evident in *David*, was replaced by a sense of vengeance against people who sinned.

It's likely that Vittoria's influence was responsible for this change. In describing the biblical story and prophecy about Jesus, she wrote, "Christ [Jesus] comes twice: the first time . . . he only shows his great kindness, his clemency and his pity. . . . The second time he comes armed and

Jeremiah was a prophet included in the Sistine Chapel ceiling. Michelangelo probably used himself as the model.

The dome at St. Peter's was Michelangelo's last big project. He did not live to see it finished. Giacomo della Porta took over and completed the construction of the dome in 1590.

shows his justice, his majesty, his grandeur and his almighty power, and there is no longer any time for pity or room for pardon."[2]

The immense figures that had stood out as individuals in the ceiling were replaced by a mass of struggling humanity. When it was unveiled in 1541, the Pope fell to his knees and begged forgiveness for his sins.

Paul quickly gave Michelangelo two more commissions. He had just built a new chapel (named for himself), and he wanted Michelangelo to create two frescoes, *The Crucifixion of St. Peter* and *The Conversion of St. Paul*. They would be Michelangelo's last paintings. Scholars do not rate them as highly as his earlier work.

Painting these frescoes did not take all of Michelangelo's time. In 1545, he finally finished the Julius tomb. He wasn't happy with it, and neither was the della Rovere family. They never moved Julius's body to the tomb. To this day, it remains empty.

In 1547, Michelangelo suffered a bitter blow when Vittoria Colonna died. He wrote one of his many poems to her, describing his grief:

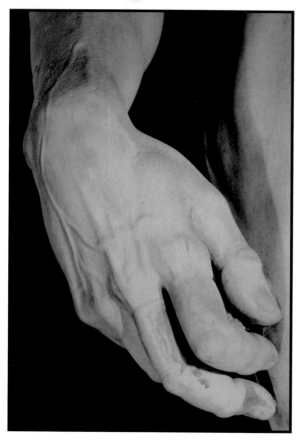

Michelangelo used his own hand as a model for David's. (Compare to the artist's hand on page 28.) The hand reveals Michelangelo's close attention to detail.

When the prime mover of many sighs
Heaven took through death from out her earthly place,
Nature, that never made so fair a face,
Remained ashamed, and tears were in all eyes.[3]

His health was continuing to decline. He sometimes thought that nothing awaited him except death.

Despite his depression and poor health, he continued to work. A friend noted, "I have seen Michelangelo . . . no longer among the most robust, knock off more chips of a very hard marble in a quarter of an hour than three young stone carvers could have done in three or four, an

almost incredible thing to one who has not seen it; and I thought the whole work would fall to pieces because he moved with such impetuosity and fury, knocking to the floor large chunks three and four fingers thick with a single blow so precisely aimed that if he had gone even minimally further than necessary, he risked losing it all."[4]

He had one more spectacular creation left in him.

Bramante hadn't been able to finish the work on St. Peter's Basilica. Neither had the succession of architects who followed him. In 1547, the Pope made Michelangelo the architect for St Peter's. Michelangelo attached one stipulation: He would receive no pay. He would undertake the work for the glory of God. Growing up in Florence, he had been greatly influenced by the city's cathedral, which featured a magnificent dome. He decided to erect a similar dome at St. Peter's.

Michelangelo's appointment unleashed a storm of protest. Many people supported the design of the most recent architect, Antonio da Sangallo the Younger. They continually attacked Michelangelo, especially when he began tearing down some of what Sangallo had already erected.

Michelangelo often became discouraged. The current duke of Florence, Cosimo de' Medici, was constantly urging him to return home. Michelangelo wrote Vasari, "I call God as a witness that, against my will, Pope Paul forced me ten years ago to work in the construction of St. Peter's. If we had continued to work in said fabric until today as we began at that time, enough progress would have been made so that I would be satisfied with it, and would be able to return to Florence. But, through work stoppages, progress slowed down, and what is more, it is slowing down as we are facing the most exhausting and difficult part; so that, if I abandoned it now, it would amount to a most shameful repudiation [rejection] of the prize which I have earned during ten years' hard work for the love of God."[5]

Other than wanting to glorify God, he may also have seen the project as a way of atoning for his sins. As he wrote his nephew Lionardo, "God entrusted me with this work."[6] It also helped that he had had the confidence of each succeeding pope.

Like so much of Michelangelo's work, St. Peter's remained unfinished at his death. In spite of his declining health, Michelangelo had continued to work on St. Peter's and other projects up until six days before his death on February 18, 1564. He was nearly ninety when he died. In his final days, he destroyed much of the work that he hadn't finished. He was a perfectionist until the end.

The Pope wanted to bury him in Rome, but Duke Cosimo de' Medici was determined that Florence would be his final resting place. He smuggled the artist's remains out of Rome. In Florence, virtually the entire city turned out to honor him.

As biographer Irving Stone notes, "By actual count, Michelangelo was kept from his beloved marble for a full half of his working life. This is why he sometimes fell into despair, and toward the end thought that he had not accomplished very much. Yet his body of work is formidable; in marble and paint, architecture, engineering and poetry, all of it so magnificently high in quality that one may be justified in thinking of him as the single greatest artist in the history of man."[7]

One measure of Michelangelo's enduring fame came in 1972. A man screamed, "I am Jesus Christ!" and attacked the *Pietà* with a sledgehammer. He knocked off several pieces before being subdued. People all over the world were shocked and horrified. It seemed to be a tragedy of epic proportions.

Careful work restored the statue to its original condition. For additional protection, the *Pietà* was placed behind bulletproof glass.

Crazed humans aren't the only enemy of Michelangelo's works. Centuries of smoke, pollution, and even human breath coated frescoes in the Sistine Chapel with a thick layer of grime. Art restoration experts spent thirteen years—more than three times as long as it took Michelangelo to paint it—to restore the ceiling to its original luster.

Countless numbers of awed onlookers can now view Michelangelo's masterpiece as he originally conceived it. It is an extremely rare person who can leave the Sistine Chapel without agreeing with Irving Stone—that Michelangelo may just be the greatest artist of all time.

St. Peter's Basilica

According to tradition, Jesus' chief disciple, St. Peter, was crucified in Rome in the year 64, during the reign of the cruel Emperor Nero. St. Peter requested that he be crucified upside down. He believed that he wasn't good enough to die in the same way that Jesus had.

In 324, Roman emperor Constantine decided to build a basilica, or church, on the site where St. Peter was reportedly buried. His remains lay directly beneath the altar of the new structure. The structure occupied the site for well over 1,000 years.

By the middle of the fifteenth century, the basilica had begun to crumble. In 1450, Pope Nicholas V made plans to rebuild it, but very little was accomplished. About thirty years later, Pope Sixtus IV had the Sistine Chapel built nearby.

The rebuilding process moved into high gear when Julius II became Pope. It seemed obvious that the grandiose tomb Michelangelo designed for him wouldn't fit into the existing structure. The pope announced a competition to design a new, much grander building that would be appropriate for the tomb. Donato Bramante was the winner. Julius laid the cornerstone in 1506 on the same site as the original basilica.

Following Bramante's death in 1514, a succession of architects made little progress until Michelangelo's appointment. After his death in 1564, it took another sixty-two years to complete the project. St. Peter's body still rests beneath the altar.

In 1667, Gianlorenzo Bernini completed construction of the colonnades that extend outward from each side of the Basilica to create St. Peter's Square. Up to 60,000 people can crowd into the square for special occasions.

For many years, St. Peter's was the largest Christian church in the world. That changed in 1990. The Basilica of Our Lady of Peace of Yamoussoukro was completed in Ivory Coast, a country in Africa. Modeled after St. Peter's, it is even larger than the original.

St. Peter's Basilica

1475	Born on March 6 at Caprese, Italy
c.1489	Begins sculptural studies with Medici family
1481	Mother dies
1488	Becomes apprentice to Domenico Ghirlandaio
c.1489	Begins sculptural studies with Medici family
c.1490	Suffers broken nose in fight with Pietro Torrigiano
1494	Flees from Florence and settles in Bologna for a year
1495	Returns to Florence; carves *Cupid*
1496	Invited by Cardinal Raffaele Riario to go to Rome
1499	Carves *Pietà*
1501	Returns to Florence, obtains contract for *David*
1504	Completes *David*
1505	Signs contract with Pope Julius II to produce his tomb
1508	Begins painting Sistine Chapel ceiling
1512	Finishes Sistine Chapel ceiling
1517	Appointed to design facade for church of San Lorenzo
1521	Begins work on Medici chapel
1524	Starts work on Laurentian Library
1529	Organizes defense of Florence
1534	Moves to Rome permanently
1535	Begins painting *Last Judgment*
1536	Meets Vittoria Colonna
1541	Completes *Last Judgment*
1545	Completes tomb of Pope Julius II
1547	Appointed chief architect of St. Peter's Basilica
1550	Finishes frescoes in Pauline Chapel
1564	Dies in Rome on February 18

1428	Influential Italian artist Masaccio dies at the age of twenty-six.
1430*	Italian sculptor Donatello completes a bronze statue of David, the first free-standing nude statue since ancient times.
1452	Leonardo da Vinci is born.
1453	Johann Gutenberg prints the Bible.
1469	Lorenzo "the Magnificent" de' Medici comes to power in Florence.
1483	First mass in the Sistine Chapel is celebrated.
1484	Sandro Botticelli begins painting *Birth of Venus*.
1492	Christopher Columbus lands in the Americas; Lorenzo de' Medici dies.
1498	Da Vinci completes *The Last Supper*.
1512	Copernicus proposes that Earth orbits the sun.
1513	Juan Ponce de Leon discovers Florida.
1517	Martin Luther begins the Protestant Reformation.
1519	Ferdinand Magellan leaves Spain on his round-the-world voyage; Raphael dies; da Vinci dies.
1543	Spanish religious leaders order the burning of Protestants.
1550	Giorgio Vasari publishes *The Lives of the Artists*.
1558	Elizabeth I becomes English queen, starting the Elizabethan Age, which becomes noted for its support of artists and writers.
1560	The Uffizi Gallery in Florence is founded; much of the artwork had been owned by the Medici family.
1561	Accademia dell'Arte del Disegno becomes the first drawing academy in Europe.
1577	English seafarer Francis Drake begins round-the-world voyage.
1588	English defeat the Spanish Armada.
1590	Giacomo della Porta completes dome of St. Peter's Basilica.
1594	Shakespeare writes *Romeo and Juliet*.
1598	Gianlorenzo Bernini is born; he becomes the next great Italian sculptor after Michelangelo.
1607	English found the colony of Jamestown, their first settlement in the Americas.
1608	Galileo Galilei builds a telescope and begins observing the heavens.

* This date is not universally accepted

CHAPTER NOTES

Chapter 1. Discovering a Genius

1. Robert Coughlan, *The World of Michelangelo* (New York: Time-Life Books, 1966), p. 12.

2. Giorgio Vasari, *Artists of the Renaissance*, translated by George Bull (New York: Viking Press, 1978), p. 233.

3. Ibid., p. 234.

4. Michelangelo Buonarroti, *I, Michelangelo, Sculptor: An Autobiography Through Letters*, edited by Irving Stone and Jean Stone, translated by Charles Speroni (New York: Doubleday and Company, 1962), pp. 8–9.

5. Vasari, p. 234.

Chapter 2. Becoming Famous

1. William E. Wallace, *Michelangelo: The Complete Sculpture, Painting, Architecture* (New York, Beaux Arts Editions, 1998); excerpt, http://www.hlla.com/reference/mb-bio.html

2. John Addington Symonds, *The Life of Michelangelo Buonarroti*. http://www.gutenberg.org/files/11242/11242-8.txt

3. Giorgio Vasari, *Artists of the Renaissance*, translated by George Bull (New York: Viking Press, 1978), p. 236.

4. Rona Goffen, *Renaissance Rivals: Michelangelo, Leonardo, Raphael, Titian* (New Haven, Connecticut: Yale University Press, 2002), p. 403.

5. Gilles Néret, *Michelangelo*, translated by Peter Snowdon (Cologne, Germany: Taschen, 2000), p. 15.

6. Kirsch, J.P. "Girolamo Savonarola." http://www.newadvent.org/cathen/13490a.htm

Chapter 3. The Sistine Chapel

1. Ross King, *Michelangelo and the Pope's Ceiling* (New York: Walker and Company, 2003), p. 9.

2. Ibid.

3. Ibid.

4. Michelangelo Buonarroti, *I, Michelangelo, Sculptor: An Autobiography Through Letters*, edited by Irving Stone and Jean Stone, translated by Charles Speroni (New York: Doubleday and Company, 1962), p. 42.

5. Robin Richmond, *Michelangelo and the Creation of the Sistine Chapel* (New York: Crescent Books, 1999), p. 50.

6. Ibid.

7. Giorgio Vasari, *Artists of the Renaissance*, translated by George Bull (New York: Viking Press, 1978), p. 258.

8. Ibid., p. 179.

Chapter 4. Defending Florence

1. William E. Wallace, *Michelangelo: The Complete Sculpture, Painting, Architecture* (New York, Beaux Arts Editions, 1998); excerpt, http://www.hlla.com/reference/mb-bio.html

2. Robert Coughlan, *The World of Michelangelo* (New York: Time-Life Books, 1966), p. 153.

3. Ibid., p. 160.

4. Edward Gibbon, *The History of the Decline and Fall of the Roman Empire*, Volume 6, Chapter 71: "Prospect of the Ruins of Rome in the Fifteenth Century," published 1788, from http://www.web-books.com/Classics/Nonfiction/History/RomanEmpire6/RomanEmpire6C13P1.htm

Chapter 5. Rome and St. Peter's

1. Giorgio Vasari, *Artists of the Renaissance*, translated by George Bull (New York: Viking Press, 1978), p. 271.

2. Robert Coughlan, *The World of Michelangelo* (New York: Time-Life Books, 1966), p. 174.

3. Michelangelo Buonarroti, "To Vittoria Colonna," translated into English by H. W. Longfellow, http://www.poetry-archive.com/b/to_vittoria_colonna.html

4. William E. Wallace, *Michelangelo: The Complete Sculpture,* *Painting, Architecture* (New York, Beaux Arts Editions, 1998); excerpt, http://www.hlla.com/reference/mb-bio.html

5. Michelangelo Buonarroti, *I, Michelangelo, Sculptor: An Autobiography Through Letters*, edited by Irving Stone and Jean Stone, translated by Charles Speroni (New York: Doubleday and Company, 1962), p. 255.

6. Ibid., p. 257.

7. Ibid., p. 276.

FURTHER READING

For Young Adults

Di Gagno, Gabriella. *Masters of Art: Michelangelo*. New York: Peter Bedrick Books, 1998.

Green, Jen. *Famous Artists: Michelangelo*. Hauppage, New York: Barron's Educational Series, 1994.

Lace, William W. *The Importance of Michelangelo*. San Diego, California: Lucent Books, 1993.

Pettet, Jayne. *Michelangelo: Genius of the Renaissance*. New York: Franklin Watts, 1998.

Somervill, Barbara A. *Michelangelo: Sculptor and Painter*. Minneapolis, Minnesota: Compass Point Books, 2005.

Stanley, Diane. *Michelangelo*. New York: HarperCollins, 2000.

Ventura, Piero. *Michelangelo's World*. Translated by Richard Pierce. New York: G.P. Putnam's Sons, 1989.

Wilkinson, Philip. *Michelangelo: The Young Artist Who Dreamed of Perfection*. Washington, D.C.: National Geographic Children's Books, 2006.

Works Consulted

Buonarroti, Michelangelo. *I, Michelangelo, Sculptor: An Autobiography Through Letters*. Edited by Irving Stone and Jean Stone. Translated by Charles Speroni. New York: Doubleday and Company, 1962.

Copplestone, Trewin. *Michelangelo*. New York: Gramercy Books, 2000.

Coughlan, Robert. *The World of Michelangelo*. New York: Time-Life Books, 1966.

Goffen, Rona. *Renaissance Rivals: Michelangelo, Leonardo, Raphael, Titian*. New Haven, Connecticut: Yale University Press, 2002.

King, Ross. *Michelangelo and the Pope's Ceiling*. New York: Walker and Company, 2003.

Néret, Gilles. *Michelangelo*. Translated by Peter Snowdon. Cologne, Germany: Taschen, 2000.

Richmond, Robin. *Michelangelo and the Creation of the Sistine Chapel*. New York: Crescent Books, 1999.

Rizzatti, Maria Luisa. *The Life Times and Art of Michelangelo*. Translated by C.J. Richards. New York: Crescent Books, 1966.

Vasari, Giorgio. *Artists of the Renaissance*. Translated by George Bull. New York: Viking Press, 1978.

On the Internet

Catholic Encyclopedia: Basilica of St. Peter's. http://www.newadvent.org/cathen/13369b.htm

The Galileo Project: The Medici Family. http://galileo.rice.edu/gal/medici.html

Gibbon, Edward. *The History of the Decline and Fall of the Roman Empire*, Volume 6, Chapter 71: "Prospect of the Ruins of Rome in the Fifteenth Century," published 1788, from http://www.web-books.com/Classics/Nonfiction/History/RomanEmpire6/RomanEmpire6C13P1.htm

Kirsch, J.P. *Girolamo Savonarola.* http://www.newadvent.org/cathen/13490a.htm

Kreis, Steven. "Girolamo Savonarola, 1452–1498." http://www.historyguide.org/intellect/savonarola.html

Museum of Science, Boston. *Leonardo da Vinci, Renaissance Man.* http://www.mos.org/leonardo/bio.html

Symonds, John Addington. *The Life of Michelangelo Buonarroti.* http://www.gutenberg.org/files/11242/11242-8.txt

Today in Odd History: Laszlo Toth, "Jesus Christ," Attacks the Pietà (May 21, 1972). http://www.newsoftheodd.com/article1024.html

Wallace, William E. Michelangelo: *The Complete Sculpture, Painting, Architecture* (New York, Beaux Arts Editions, 1998); excerpt, http://www.hlla.com/reference/mb-bio.html

apprentice (uh-PREN-tis)—A person bound to a skilled craftsman for a certain period of time in order to learn that craft.

aristocratic (uh-RIS-tuh-KRAA-tik)—Of the upper class of nobles.

atoning (uh-TOH-ning)—Making up for.

banal (buh-NAL)—Commonplace, very ordinary.

basilica (buh-SIH-lih-kuh)—A Catholic church with ceremonial privileges.

biblical (BIH-blih-kul)—Relating to the Jewish Bible (Old Testament) or to the Christian Bible (Old and New Testaments).

cadaver (kuh-DAA-ver)—A corpse; dead body.

city-state—A city and surrounding countryside which acts as a small country.

classical (KLAA-sih-kul)—Relating to ancient Greece and Rome.

clemency (KLEH-mun-see)—Mercy, forgiveness.

commission (kuh-MIH-shun)—An agreement to create a piece of art and be paid for it in installments, including a sum at completion.

excommunicate (eks-kuh-MYOO-nih-kayt)—To declare a person can no longer be part of a church.

fresco (FRES-koh)—A painting done on wet plaster; the plaster absorbs the paint and dries with it, giving depth and richness to the piece.

humanism (HYOO-mah-nih-zum)—A belief in the importance of non-religious matters and in the ability of the human mind to solve problems.

impetuosity (im-peh-choo-WAH-sih-tee)—Impulsiveness; acting out of passion instead of reason.

obelisks (AH-buh-lisks)—Tall, slender monuments that usually have four sides and are topped with a pyramid.

papacy (PAY-puh-see)—The office of the Pope (the leader of the Roman Catholic Church).

prior (PRY-ur)—A leader of a religious community such as a monastery.

prophet (PRAH-fet)—A person who makes predictions about the future.

sacristy (SAA-kruh-stee)—An area in a church where sacred objects are kept and priests put on their robes.

salvation (sal-VAY-shun)—In the Christian religion, being saved from the power and effects of sin.

INDEX

Adrian VI, Pope   30
Bernini, Gianlorenzo   41
Bramante, Donato   24, 25, 33, 39, 41
Buonarroti, Buonarroto (brother)   10, 32
Buonarroti, Francesca (mother)   7, 9, 10
Buonarriti, Giovansimone (brother)   10
Buonarroti, Lodovico (father)   7, 9, 10, 11,
     12, 20, 32
Buonarroti, Michelangelo
     apprenticed to Ghirlandaio   11–12
     becomes St. Peter's architect   37–38
     birth of   9, 10
     childhood of   10–11
     death of   39–40, 41
     defends Florence   31–32
     and dissections   17–18
     education of   11, 12, 16–18
     in Medici household   16
     nose broken   16–17
     poetry of   38
     Pope Julius II and   23–26
     moves to Rome   19
     studies sculpture   15–16
     works of
         Bacchus   18, 19
         Battle of the Centaurs   17
         Church of San Lorenzo   29
         Conversion of St. Paul   37
         Crucifixion of St. Peter   37
         Cupid   19
         David   8, 19–20, 23, 36, 38
         Giuliano de' Medici   13
         The Last Judgment   31, 36
         Laurentian Library   30
         Madonna and Child   6
         Madonna of the Stairs   17
         Medici chapel and tombs   30
         Moses   26, 34
         Pietà   14, 19, 39, 40
         River God (study)   16
         St. Peter's Basilica   36, 37–39
         Self-Portrait   28, 31, 38

Sistine Chapel   22, 24, 25–26, 30, 31,
     36, 37, 40, 41
     sketches   11
     statue of Julius II   25
     Tomb of Julius II   23–24, 26, 29, 30,
         32, 34, 35, 37, 41
Buonarroti, Sigismondo (brother)   10
Cavalieri, Tommaso de   35
Charles V, Emperor   30–31
Clement VII, Pope   13, 30, 31, 32, 36
Colonna, Vittoria   35, 36, 37
Donatello   15
Duccio, Agostino di   19
Francis I, King   27, 30
Ghirlandaio, Dominico   11, 12, 16
Giotto   16
Granacci, Francesco   11
Julius II, Pope   23–26, 29, 33, 41
Leo X, Pope   13, 29–30
Leonardo da Vinci   15, 23, 27
Masaccio   16, 17
Medici, Allesandro de'   13, 32
Medici, Cosimo de'   13, 39, 40
Medici, Giovanni di Lorenzo de' (see Leo X)
Medici, Guiliano de'   13, 30
Medici, Lorenzo de'   12, 13, 15, 16, 17, 18, 21
Medici, Lorenzo di Pierfrancesco de'   18–19
Medici, Piero de'   17, 18, 21
Paul III, Pope   35, 36, 37
Peter, Saint   41
Poggius   33
Raphael   25, 33
Renaissance   10, 13, 23
Riario, Cardinal Raffaele   18
Sangallo the Younger, Antonio da   39
St. Peter's Basilica   24, 25, 36, 39, 41
Savonarola, Girolamo   18, 21
Sixtus IV, Pope   41
Torrigiano, Pietro   16–17
Vasari, Giorgio   9, 10, 26, 27